Stefan George

by ULRICH K. GOLDSMITH

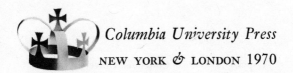

Columbia University Press
NEW YORK & LONDON 1970

ULRICH K. GOLDSMITH is chairman of the Program in Comparative Literature at the University of Colorado. He is the author of *Stefan George: A Study of His Early Work.*

for B. B. G.

Copyright © 1970 Columbia University Press
SBN: 231-03204-3
Library of Congress Catalog Card Number: 78-110601
Printed in the United States of America

Acknowledgment is made to Verlag Helmut Küpper, formerly Georg Bondi, Düsseldorf and Munich, for permission to quote from the two-volume edition of Stefan George's *Werke* published in 1968.

Stefan George

For five months in 1968, on the occasion of the one hundredth anniversary of Stefan George's birth, the German Literary Archives in the Schiller Museum at Marbach held a unique exhibition of some 500 literary and pictorial documents in his honor. Manuscripts and first editions of his own work formed the lesser part of the exhibition; his poetic output was relatively small. The two volumes of the complete edition of 1958 comprise only about 600 pages of his own poetry and 60 pages of prose writings; the remaining 500 pages contain translations from other poets (Baudelaire's *Fleurs du mal*, Shakespeare's *Sonnets*, and selections from Dante's *Divina Commedia* forming the bulk). What made the exhibition unique and what would have pleased George is the fact that it included a great variety of materials stemming from the circle of his friends, the so-called *George-Kreis*: writers, poets, and scholars who had been influenced or trained by him. They and their descendants have had no mean share in the preservation of the memory of Stefan George. This situation offers an ironic contrast to the one hundredth anniversary of the birth of Germany's greatest poet in 1849: Goethe's fame was then in its darkest eclipse. George's work lacks facile popular appeal as much as does *Faust, Part II* or the *West-eastern Divan*, but he has not suffered such a long period of neglect as Goethe did. Our knowledge of his background and that of the numerous men and—fewer—women around him has recently been enriched by several volumes of correspondence and reminiscences, and a number of notable monographs give evidence of the resurgence of serious interest among younger scholars after it had ebbed during the first fifteen years subsequent to the collapse of the "Third Reich." The study of George has become part of the West German high school and university curriculums.

Whereas Goethe's universal reputation was established beyond doubt by 1949 and is no longer dependent on the winds of change or reaction in his homeland, it is too early to speculate on the shape which George's image at home or abroad will have a hundred years hence. Its outlines are still blurred and uncertain. A dispassionate assessment of the artistic accomplishment of Stefan George will be difficult for some time to come. His work and person are not easily separable. One peculiar problem facing the critic is that the time-bound elements of his career have not been sublimated and objectified in the body of his work. He himself would probably not have regarded his pedagogic mission as being completely embodied in his poetry. He wrote no poems during the last five years of his life, but continued in his direct bid for spiritual power in the informal training of a group of disciples who were to form the core of a cultural renewal.

Those who knew and revered him called him "Master"; they were agreed that a magic power issued from his person "which inspired fear and reverence and which could only be counterbalanced by love" (Friedrich Wolters). There were others who took an instinctive dislike to what seemed to them a solemn severity and hierarchical pose, a pose that became even more distasteful when it was imitated by some of the disciples. No one denied that Stefan George had a commanding presence, a probing glance, an impressive countenance, and a superior intelligence. We are told the young George felt that in a former life he had been a royal personage; in his middle years his

[4]

bearing led some to take him for a reincarnation of Dante Alighieri.

During the Wilhelmine era almost all German writers and poets of rank were in some measure critical of the establishment and its imperial ambitions, but no one was more uncompromising and near-contemptuous in his opposition than George. In an examination of his poetry his refusal to interact with his society on any terms other than his own will have to form part of the discussion.

Ever since George's first publication (*Hymnen*, 100 copies, privately printed, 1890) his poetry and his person have been the subject of speculation and controversy. It seemed that, while he shared with the naturalists a disdain for the stale and mediocre level to which German art had sunk since the death of Goethe, his approach was that of the aesthete and practitioner of *l'art pour l'art*, remote from public concerns: "Out to the river! . . . rest in the grass, be overwhelmed/ By strong primeval scent, shunning disturbing thought" ("Weihe" [Initiation], first of the *Hymnen*). Yet by the end of the decade it became clear that his noninvolvement was not mere escape but that a fervent sense of mission was behind it. A positive approach had to be preceded by a wholesale rejection. George said later to Ernst Robert Curtius, "But the nineteenth century is fundamentally corrupt, it must be rejected radically. The idea of progress through science is madness. In all great epochs men knew that knowledge is meant only for the few and can only be communicated step by step." George wanted to bring about a moral and cultural rebirth of Germany and make her the leading nation of Europe. It was to be an educative process along the lines of the Platonic Academy. It had to begin with an elite of young men who themselves would become leaders and educators, but ultimately he demanded "from everybody,

[5]

be he poor or rich, stupid or clever, that he become different" (in conversation with Kurt Breysig, the historian, in 1916). The fact that all this was to happen through art (poetry in particular) indicates, on the one hand, how quixotic and problematic was the poet's relation to, and concept of, reality. On the other hand, it stresses the absoluteness of his claim. The story is told that once, when George was a little boy, he was left alone in the house. He went and locked all the rooms and buried the keys in the garden. "That way he made himself master of the house" (*Ewiger Augenblick*, by Robert Boehringer, 1965). Stefan George wanted to begin at the beginning, a trait not uncommon among Germans, who as a nation have labored so long and so tortuously in their search for identity. Curtius remarked, with reference to George, that "at the root of every great work of the German mind there is an absolute beginning."

Stefan George lived and died as a free-lance poet and writer, if his aloofness from all public office and private employment can be thus described. He was entirely independent of family ties. Although his room at his parents' house in Bingen was always ready for him he never cared to stay there for great lengths of time. He had no other permanent domicile but stayed, for varying periods of time, with friends in Berlin, Munich, Basel, or in a pension in Heidelberg. The only public honor which he did not decline was the Goethe Prize of the city of Frankfurt in 1927, when he was sixty. In July, 1933, the newly installed Nazi government, through its Ministry of "Culture," founded a German Poets Academy and wanted Stefan George to grace it as its first president. They were willing to put up an annual Stefan-George-Prize as an emolument for the poet or for anyone he cared to select. His young friend Ernst Morwitz, who served as his amanuensis, personally delivered the poet's answer in which he declined unequivocally. His last sentence is supposed to have read, "It is true, I am the ancestor of every national movement, but how the spirit (*Geist*) is to enter politics—that I cannot tell you." One month later George left Germany. An old physical ailment struck with redoubled force. He died in Minusio, Switzerland, on December 4, 1933.

Stefan George is said to have begun writing verse when he was a little boy. At the age of seven he invented his own secret language, an experiment he was to repeat at least twice more before he was twenty. Only two apparently indecipherable lines from the last and most elaborate of these inventions—a kind of streamlined romance language—are preserved. They form the conclusion of his poem "Ursprünge" (Origins, 1904):

> In incantations which none comprehended
> We were the sovereigns and ruled the All.
> Sweet and impelling as Attica's choros
> Over the islands and hills we sang:
> CO BESOSO PASOJE PTOROS
> CO ES ON HAMA PASOJE BOAÑ.

The poet's great-grandfather had emigrated from France (Département de la Moselle) to the right bank of the Rhine (Büdesheim, opposite Bingen). His son Stephan became a vineyard owner and member of the regional parliament. Stephan's grandson was named after him, but the French equivalent of Stefan—Étienne—was the more frequently used alternative by which he was known until he was well over twenty and felt reconciled to being a German. The family name was locally pronounced "Schorsch"; at home, French was spoken as much as German. Later, in retrospect, George emphasized that his homeland was that of the Franks, that is, the realm of Charlemagne, and he referred to the grandfather's "praise of the ever young/ and generous earth whose glory warmed him/ and whose anguish, though from a distance, caused him tears" ("Franken," 1902–3).

George was not a child prodigy. His early German verse, which he was careful not to publish until he had a right to believe that his stature was established, shows nothing resembling the precocious perfection of the poems of Loris—the nom de plume of the sixteen-year-old Hugo von Hofmannsthal. A self-conscious awkwardness marks George's juvenilia, which he entitled *Die Fibel* (The Primer, 1900). There seems to be some justification in regarding this as evidence of a childhood trauma, due to his bilingualism and all it entailed culturally. George said to Curtius, "There was a moment when I was faced with the decision as to whether to become a German poet or a French one." His case is analogous to that of the Swiss poet C. F. Meyer who had been unable to make up his mind to write in German until the Germans covered themselves with military glory and achieved political unification through the war with France in 1870–71. The factors determining George's decision twenty years later were ironically different: the new German Empire disgusted the sensitive Rhinelander through its materialistic vulgarity and artistic and intellectual mediocrity. The realities of the German scene appeared to him paltry and inimical. They drove him to travel abroad for nearly two years after he was graduated from the Gymnasium in Darmstadt: London, Switzerland, northern Italy, Paris, Spain, Copenhagen, and finally Paris again. His sojourn in the French capital and his participation in the famous *mardis soirs* of Stéphane Mallarmé have sometimes been represented as the means by which the Symbolist movement spread to the German-speaking world. This is not entirely correct. The work of Charles Baudelaire,

[8]

Mallarmé, and the Symbolists was received by the Germans rather slowly, it is true, but the process began without George and before his Parisian experience. Morover, it is erroneous to identify George's work and views, except for some aspects of the early poems, with the basic philosophy of the major Symbolist figures. What inspired the young George and made him return to his own country with the firm resolve to be a German poet was the primacy of euphony and formal perfection as it was upheld by his French *confrères;* the esteem in which the poet's vocation was held in France; the noble living example of *le Maître*, Mallarmé; and the express blessing and commission with which his French friends sent him off: to bring about a renewal of poetry and art in Germany. This amounted to a reaffirmation of George's own aspiration and will to (spiritual!) power.

The encouragement he had received was decisive. He began to gather like-minded friends about him and founded the review *Blätter für die Kunst* (Pages for Art) not long afterwards. The name of the magazine was evidently borrowed from the French *Écrits pour l'art*. As co-editor he chose Carl August Klein and as place of publication the German capital, which he loathed, but recognized as one of the "great highways." His concept of the "new art," however, differed from symbolist aesthethics. It was not metaphysically oriented, with the implication that the signs of the phenomenal world have their correspondences in the ideal realm as well as among themselves. In the first issue of the *Blätter* (October, 1892) C. A. Klein pointed out that literary epochs did not run exactly parallel in the two countries and insisted that George had to seek a path of his own, because "the perfection of the 'Parnasse' which we have not yet attained is, as a point of view, already outdated over there." Since an innovator in German poetry had

[9]

to direct his efforts against post-romantic egocentricity and sentimental mediocrity as well as against the lusterless, formless products of naturalism it was, indeed, precision in formulation and adherence to strict formal patterns which distinguished George's work from the outset. Such traits as the mystic, oracular, and reflective tendencies of symbolism are absent. This does not mean that the calculated compactness of George's work does not have its linguistic obscurities and syntactic complexities, but these are not due to the vague suggestiveness of undecipherable private symbols. The cult of artistic perfection, the erudition which evokes different periods of history or elements of the artistic national heritage, and which preceded the Symbolist movement in France, were what George saw as the foremost needs of the German poetic language. So he led German metrics back to the rules of classical prosody at a time when the Symbolists began to fight for the freedom of verse. In 1894 he wrote, "Free verse means as much as 'white blackness'; let him who cannot move well in rhythm stride along unbound," and "The value of poetry is determined not by meaning (then it would be wisdom or erudition), but by form." He then proceeds to define form as something not merely external but as "that deeply moving element in rhythm and sound, by which at all time the originators, the Masters, have distinguished themselves from the epigones, the artists of second rank." While this is not a satisfactory definition of "form" it should make clear that for George, at this stage, at least, sound came before sense.

It was in Paris that George was introduced to the poetry of Baudelaire and was so profoundly impressed that he began immediately to translate it into German. In 1891 he published 115 of the 151 poems of *Les Fleurs du mal* as *Die Blumen des Bösen*. The work is remarkable for the bold originality in the euphonious handling of the German language, and, especially,

[10]

for the light that is thrown by the poet's translation technique on his own conception of poetry. There is justification for saying that in Baudelaire George searched for himself. In so doing he misunderstood him in some important aspects. A few hints must suffice here. The motive of spleen which permeates the French work from beginning to end is suppressed or eliminated by the translator. The crucial first poem, the apostrophe "To the Reader," is absent from the translation. The title of the first part of *Les Fleurs du mal*, "Spleen et idéal," is rendered as "Trübsinn und Vergeistigung," which means approximately "Dreariness and Spiritualization." Thus the fundamental dualism of human existence as the French poet saw it is bridged by the activating implication of "spiritualization." Moreover, George practices a kind of censorship in that he omits whole poems, or tones down expressions, which refer to details of crude physical and erotic realities. He wants to see Baudelaire as the poet of "fervent spirituality." A closer examination of *Die Blumen des Bösen* shows, furthermore, an extraordinary reduction in the variety and number of Baudelaire's images, due to a shortening of the lines; in place of the original's alexandrines we find iambic pentameter. One of George's maxims was "rein ellenmässig: die kürze" ("in terms of inches simply: brevity"). There is a strong tendency in George to fashion the line of verse as a basic unit. Consequently the translation is, by comparison with the original, pithy and apodictic, and, at times, syntactically overcomplicated. Finally, and this is again related to the reduction in length, the comparison shows that the translation—parts of which are indeed brilliantly skillful—often does violence to the images of the original in such a manner that sense is sacrificed for the sake of sound.

In George's work, insistence on formal conciseness serves the purpose of a strict control of emotion. One can sense the poet's urge to challenge and revolutionize, but also a deep

[11]

Nach dem segentag· sie kehren
Heim zum dorf in stillgebeten·
DIE bein fernen gott der lehren·
DIE schon bei dem naherflehten.

Kam ein pfiff am grund entlang?
Alle lampen flackern bang.
War es nicht als ob es riefe?
Es empfingen ihre bräute
Schwarze knaben aus der tiefe . .
Glocke läute glocke läute!

(Windmill cease to move your arms
Since the heath desires rest.
Ponds expect a thawing wind.
Guarding them are shimmering lances
And the little trees are rigid
Like a white-washed gorse-bush cluster.

Gently gliding white-clad children
Cross the lake on clouded ice
After being blessed they now turn
Toward their village stilly praying
To the distant god of dogma
Or to their adored redeemer.

Did a whistle graze the ground?
Anxious flickering shakes all lights.
Was there not a call from someone?
Youths all black, from deep below,
Fast arose to take their brides . .
Bell ring out, ring bell, ring out!)

The difficulties accompanying the presentation of George's
poetic art in translation (especially when analysis and interpre-
tation are attempted) are well-nigh insurmountable. The
English versions given here aim only at communicating the
meaning, the meter, and the general tone. The rhyme has been
sacrificed, as have other subtleties of euphony. Lines 4 and
14 of the original "Mühle . . ." poem cause one to speculate

about the reason for the use of "lanzen" and "lampen." The preciousness of the word *lances*, when it refers to "reeds," is probably not due to an expressionistic urge but rather to a need for vowel euphony, while *lamps*, which could refer to candles in the children's hands or to the lights on the shore or to both, may very well be used solely to complete the *a-e* pattern throughout the line.

The book *Algabal* followed quickly upon *Pilgerfahrten*. Inability to come to terms with the world of man because it falls short of the poetic dream can be turned into rebellious opposition to reality. The humility of the pilgrim is transformed into a wishdream of power and amorality, as embodied in the figure of a solipsistic late Roman emperor. The transition between the two books is the last pilgrim poem, entitled "Die Spange" (The Link):

> I wanted it of coolest iron
> And fashioned like a firm smooth band.
> Yet all the mountain's shafts were barren,
> Had no such metal for the mold.
>
> Different now it shall be made.
> Like a great and wondrous cluster:
> Of gold which is as red as fire,
> Of richest sparkling precious stones.

George's emperor Algabal is a symbolic figure rather than a historical personage, although it is not difficult to recognize features which he has in common with the boy emperor Heliogabalus of the early third century A.D., with literary treatments Heliogabalus received at the hands of French *décadents* and symbolist authors, and with King Ludwig II of Bavaria. The book bears an inscription to Ludwig's memory, as addressed to him by his "younger brother," Algabal. Again the poetry does not present factual accounts, but conveys the splendor of the artificial, sunless, non- or antinatural subterranean realm which Algabal has created for himself. Here the deified emporer's power and profligacy are as absolute as his yearning for beauty. However, he is a figure of tragic isolation. The most famous poem of the book is that of the great black flower which conveys Algabal's disillusionment with his fantastic schemes which used to (but can no more?) make him forget *Sorge* (care):

> My garden requires no warmth. It is airless,
> The garden which I have built as my own,
> And the swarms of lifeless birds which it harbors
> Have never beheld yet the blossoms of spring.
>
> Of charcoal the tree trunks, of charcoal the branches,
> And gloomy the fields within borders of gloom.
> The boughs are full-laden with fruit never gathered
> And gleam like lava in groves of pine.
>
> A grayish glow from a hidden hollow
> Betrays not when morning or evening nears
> And dusty vapors from oil of almond
> Hover above the crops and the leas.
>
> But how, in my sanctuary, shall I create thee
> —I asked when brooding I walked through this realm,
> In bold speculations oblivious of care—
> Wondrous flower, great and black?

The symbol of the black flower here is antiromantic, that is, it is pointedly not a dream symbol like Novalis's blue flower or Baudelaire's "black tulip, blue Dahlia" of the "Pays de Cocagne." Algabal "is concentrating on a complete reversal of the natural which is to culminate in the artificial production of an organic form" (Ernst Morwitz in a letter to the author

[15]

of the present essay), that is, in the willed creation of a large flower that possesses a color not found in nature.

The poetry of the *Algabal* cycle is an example of artifice turned into art. However, it does not spring from an "art for art's sake" concept. The poet's distance from reality does not mean that he does not wish to relate to it. While he does not and cannot, at this point, address himself directly in his poetry to the problems of his age, he is delivering a challenge in the guise of an immoralist. George is reported to have said, "*Algabal* is a revolutionary book."

He supervised its printing in Paris in September, 1892, and went home to Bingen: ill. It is safe to assume that what he lightly referred to as "the weakness of nerves from which each of us suffers a little" was a period of physical exhaustion and inner conflict which he was loath to discuss with anyone.

Great attention was paid by George to the cyclical order of the poems in every one of his works. The preferred order was tripartite and was first used in *Algabal.* The three parts of the book are "Im Unterreich" (In the Subterranean Realm), "Tage" (Days), and "Andenken" (Memories). The four poems of "Im Unterreich" convey the luxurious and artificial splendor of the emperor's present surroundings. In the ten poems of the second part some of his actions and reactions are evoked, all ominously pervaded by an atmosphere of crime and menace. All but two of the poems are written in the first-person singular. In the ninth of these Algabal hears noises of an impending palace revolt by "the herd that forgets to obey" and resolves to anticipate his "Ides of March" by a self-inflicted demise. He does not tell us, needless to say, whether he carried out the resolve; in the next poem he hears the sound of enchanting Syrian music from above ground and wonders whether to chase the musicians away or whether to yield to the temptation

[16]

to remain among the living. Since this is the end of "Tage," to be followed by "Memories," all spoken by the emperor in person, the reader has to forgo the satisfaction of hearing the end of the "story." Seven poems form the "Memories," narcissistic reflections of feelings and events from the emperor's youth, such as his elevation to throne and divinity by the victorious Roman soldiery who were under the spell of his boyish beauty, his poisoning of two children in their sleep, and an early death wish ("Gloomy comforter, son of the night"). The book has one more poem, under the title of "Vogelschau" (Augury). It is outside the Algabal cycle, the lyrical "I" being the poet speaking of the next phase of his work. He sees white swallows fly again "in the wind so cold and clear!" after the exotic parrots and hummingbirds which "flitted through the wonder-trees/ in the forest of tusferi" have vanished. The return to a calmer, cooler poetry is thus augured.

The next two volumes of poetry share a general tone of calmness variously felt as serenity, subdued tension, or delicate melancholy. The one was published (privately, 200 copies) in 1895 under the lengthy threefold title of *Die Bücher der Hirten- und Preisgedichte, der Sagen und Sänge und der hängenden Gärten* (The Books of Eclogues and Eulogies, of Legends and Lays, and of the Hanging Gardens). The other, called *Das Jahr der Seele* (The Year of the Soul), appeared in 1897. No sharp chronological dividing line separates the individual poems of the two cycles. The publication of *Das Jahr der Seele* was being planned when *Die Bücher* . . . was at the printer's, as we know from a letter George wrote to his Bingen friend Ida Coblenz sometime in 1895 and in which he speaks of a "turning point" in his life and is "looking back upon a whole life which, I feel, is being replaced by an entirely different one. I want to end it with the publication of my

[17]

books." He then mentions that *Hymnen, Pilgerfahrten*, and *Algabal* are to be in the first volume, *Die Bücher . . .* in the second, and that "the latest poems" are to be published as *Annum* [sic] *animae* or *Das Jahr der Seele* in the third. These were to be regular public editions, available through the book trade. Everything that he had put out hitherto had appeared in private editions of 100 to 200 copies, owing to both limited demand and limited funds. Actually *Das Jahr . . .* had also to be published privately first (200 copies), in 1897. It was not until 1899 that the three books appeared as planned.

The short preface to *Die Bücher . . .* implies that the poet intended to put an end to romantic historicizing and to the glorification of the past in poetry. His books are to contain motifs and reflections of the three great realms of Antiquity, the Middle Ages, and the Orient in so far as his modern consciousness produces a live response to them. In his own words: "Of the great realms of our civilization, no more is contained here than what is still alive in some of us."

The craftsmanship practiced to this end is subtle. The poet does not merely evoke the original themes to which his "soul" responds. The motifs, while traceable to erudite sources or previous poetic treatment, are transformed by a modern sensibility. All of the fourteen *Hirtengedichte* are rhymeless, all but two are nonstanzaic. The meter is predominantly iambic with five feet in some poems, six in others. Two are in hexameters. No strictly Greek metric patterns are used. The first three poems consist of 9, 10, and 10 serene and stately lines respectively and deal with the relationship of two maidens who share the fate of having lost their betrothed on the same day, a loss that marked the beginning of their friendship. They spend each anniversary of the day in reminiscing and walking together to the well to fetch water, until after seven years one of them senses behind her "sister's" quiet happiness a pre-occupation with a new "secret": from behind the vine-covered fence she expects someone to come and carry her away. The transfigured simplicity of the theme is ingratiatingly deceptive. The sparse and calmly measured words are certainly similar to some Alcaic or Sapphic strophes. However, the fact that the water pitchers are made of gray clay and that there are two poplars and a pine tree by the well show that the locale is not meant to be identified as Mediterranean. Moreover, one must not overlook the symbolism of the trees: if we take the poplars to stand for the girls, the one pine indicates that the betrothed was one and the same man. Similarly, the young hero of "Tag des Hirten" is not simply an untutored ancient shepherd. Enjoying the fine spring weather, he abandons his flock to wander through a cool valley with rushing mountain streams, goes to sleep in the forest, and, in the evening, climbs a peak to admire the sunset, "crowning . . . himself with holy leaves." In other words, he is rather like an enthusiastic young poet in the vicinity of the Rhine, leaving "the herd" behind to rise above the everyday world. The poem "Der Herr der Insel" (The Lord of the Island), in the same group and written in blank verse, tells a beautiful fable which allows no optimistic conclusion about the fate and function of the poet in the modern world. The "Lord" of the title is a great bird with purple plumage who "when rising in low and heavy flight . . . looked like a somber cloud." At night he dwells on the beach and attracts the dolphins with his song. Thus he has lived from the beginning of creation and has only been seen by the ship-wrecked. When one day "the white sails of men" approached in order to land he rose and, after surveying his territory once more, opened his great wings and "departed" (i.e., from this life), uttering "subdued notes of pain." The resemblance of

[19]

this bird to Baudelaire's "Albatross" is evident, but the Symbolist's image for the *poète maudit* is that of a pitiful sufferer who was mocked by the sailors as Christ was by the soldiers, whereas the Lord of the Island vanishes without losing an ounce of his dignity. One cannot but be reminded of the report that, when Germany lost World War I and there was, for a while, the danger that the Bolshevists might take over the country, George carried poison with him. In 1933, soon after Hitler had come to power, the poet left quietly for Switzerland.

The eleven *Preisgedichte* are addressed to "young men and women of this time" each of whom is given a Greek pseudonym. Two, for instance, are superscribed *An Menippa*, which stands for Ida Coblenz. Among the others addressed are the two young Belgian poets, Edmond Rassenfosse and Paul Gérardy; the Frenchman Albert Saint-Paul, who had introduced George to the *Fleurs du mal* and to Mallarmé's Tuesday evenings; the Polish poet Waclaw Lieder, some of whose poems George translated into German; and the philosopher-psychologist-graphologist Ludwig Klages, whom the poet had met in Munich and about whom more will have to be said later. The poems, mostly characterizations, memories, and admonitions, are early evidence of the pedagogical *eros* at work.

The middle book of the volume, the *Sagen und Sänge*, reflects George's knowledge of and feeling for the Middle Ages. The first rather lengthy rhymed poem bears the title "Sporenwache," which means the prayerful night vigil before the dubbing of a knight. It presents a young nobleman alone in the candle-lit chapel where a valiant ancestor lies buried. Details of the chapel, the tomb, and the knight's attire are authentically pictured. His meditations, told in the first-person singular, reveal his *état d'âme* before the final heroic dedication: thoughts of a golden-haired maiden cross his mind. He is upset by that tempting vision. Fortunately, his glance lights upon the figure of the Redeemer who is sitting on the Virgin's lap, with outstretched arms, whereupon he vows total allegiance to service in the army of his Lord. It is easy to discern here the poet's respect for, and idealization of, an individual's dedication to a high ethical purpose with a touch of the ascetic. However, George's predilection for ritual and for the solemnity of cult as such is equally important, as is the poet's original touch of ending the poem with a miracle: a covey of winged heads of angels flies up from the altar. None of the poems of *Sagen und Sänge* should be taken as personal confessions; they are imaginative poetic creations. Thus also the poem "Vom Ritter der sich verliegt" (The Knight Who Lies Idly) exists for its own sake; it is a virtuoso piece of sound images:

> Do I hear a muffled clatter?
> Fighters harnessing their horses?
> Anxious calls from balconies?
> Lances whirring?
>
> It was but a clanging gate.
>
> Do I hear the guests rejoicing?
> Busy servants, castle-stewards
> Under vine-decked galleries?
> Happy sentries?
>
> Did not someone gently waken
> Tender strings to praise the fairest
> Distant times which unsuspecting
> Shyly glided by?
>
> It was but a clanging gate.

Only the title and the first of the three stanzas rendering the knight's acoustic deceptions have a specifically medieval flavor.

A more personal involvement informs the poem "Frauenlob." The title refers to the late medieval poet, and the first of the "Meistersinger," Heinrich von Meissen, who had earned his sobriquet through his varied and unending praise of women in his song. At his funeral a large crowd of women is said to have wept for him and to have poured "choicest wines, flowers, and jewels" into his grave. George presents Frauenlob's devotion to women as ever unrequited, hence the offerings after his death form a bitter contrast. This again expresses the disillusioned and sometimes sentimentalized view which the young poets of the late nineteenth century took of themselves and their lonely position vis-à-vis modern society.

A group of fifteen poems forms the second part of this middle book, under the title of *Sänge eines fahrenden Spielmanns* (Songs of a Wandering Minstrel): they include restrained and tender wooing notes sounded by the minstrel who will be satisfied by a loving gesture on the part of the adored lady, or the soliloquy of the highborn girl who threw a ring to the fiddler but is prepared to face reality if he should forget her. One of the finest "songs" consists of three melancholy stanzas in which the minstrel-poet expresses fatherly anxiety in the face of the inexorable realities of life and decides to leave the beloved "child":

> See, my child, I go now.
> For you must not know,
> I must never name,
> Man's distress and pain.
>
> I am grieving for you
> See, my child, I go.
> From your cheek the fragrance
> Must not blow away.
>
> I would have to speak of
> Things which will give hurt,

I would feel much anguish.
See, my child, I go.

The third of the cultural realms that nurtured the poet's soul is the Orient. George knew and loved *The Arabian Nights' Entertainments* from childhood and continued to be fascinated by the Near and Far East all through his life. He knew Wieland's *Oberon* and Goethe's *West-östlicher Divan*.

Whereas Wieland's approach to the Orient, in the opening lines of his epic poem *Oberon*, is a learned one—he asks the Muses to saddle the Hippogriff for his "ride to the old land of romances"—George enters directly and swiftly the land that was his own. He rides a magic horse which is like El Borak, the fabled steed the angel Gabriel had given to Mohammed so that he could, even in his lifetime, instantly traverse the seven heavenly spheres to visit Paradise. The short opening poem of the *Hängende Gärten* says:

> Wir werden noch einmal zum lande fliegen
> Das dir von früh auf eigen war:
> Du musst dich an den hals des zelters schmiegen·
> Du drückst an seinen zäumen den rubin
> In einer heissen nacht und ohne fahr
> Gelangst du hin.
>
> (We now shall fly to repossess the land
> That was your own from early days:
> You must hold closely to the palfrey's neck
> And press the magic ruby on the rein.
> Then safely faring through one fevered night
> You will arrive.)

During the time when George was writing this book his acquaintance with Ida Coblenz had developed into friendship. She had reacted to his poetry with remarkable perception and was especially fond of what she called the "Semiramis-Lieder."

She said many years later that they were written for her. It would be erroneous to designate this or any other personal experience as the source of the matter of these poems, but the lyrical "I" is obviously not as alone and removed from the world as the lyrical "I" of *Algabal*. Characteristically, the lyrical subject in the *Hängende Gärten* is again a ruler, one who has felt predestined for kingship from his childhood days, as is recalled in the sixth poem, "Kindliches Königtum" (Childhood Kingdom). He remembers vividly the days when "In distant valleys hidden you created/ Your state in serried bushes' secrecy . . ." and when "The comrades whom your glance enflamed for you/ Felt honored by your coin and grant of lands." The oriental master-servant relationship appealed to George.

"Kindliches Königtum" contains the earliest occurrence of the word *staat* (state) in the sense of a group of faithful followers. The idea of devoted service and voluntary submission of the will to the Master's greater insight is at the core of George's later thinking and practice in the gathering of an elite around him. In 1930 the historian Friedrich Wolters published a 590-page book entitled *Stefan George und die Blätter für die Kunst: Deutsche Geistesgeschichte seit 1890* (. . . German Intellectual History since 1890). The presumptuous note in the subtitle is hard to miss.

However, the *Buch der hängenden Gärten* is poetry and it moves in a purely fairy-tale atmosphere. The returning ruler conquers the enemy's city and enters it in a conciliatory spirit. He then yields to pleasure and luxury and forgets the active life in his splendid palace. The tortuous tensions of Algabal are absent, but the real world seems like a delusion. The mood of the poem that ends the first section (of ten poems), "Friedensabend" (Peaceful Evening), reminds one of the "Knight Who

Lies Idly." The succeeding fifteen nonstanzaic love poems of between 7 and 14 lines each are the *Hängende Gärten* proper, although the title is probably meant to suggest a dreamlike state between reality and illusion and is not a direct allusion to the legendary terraced gardens of the famous Babylonian queen. The suspense of longing anxiety and passion is evoked by dense and stately language. There is, in at least two poems, the suggestion of fever heat in the garden, but this is emotional rather than physical or climatic. A close look at the details of the vegetation reveals that we are not necessarily in a Persian or Arabic landscape. The one mention of palm trees and the white sand outside the city does indeed suggest a southern or eastern climate, but otherwise we have purple-black thorn, "velvet-plumed fern," clumps of centaury, bluebells, silver willows, and fishponds, which clearly include European flora and fauna. The final poem of this section speaks of separation and termination through powerful nature symbols:

> Pale and brittle is the fishpond's glass
> And I step amiss in withered grass.
> Palms with pointed fingers prick me.
> Weary leaves in hissing turmoil
> Jerkily are chased by unseen hands
> All around our Eden's fallow walls.
> The night is overcast and close.

Part three of the Book deals with the end of the dream kingdom. The ruler finds he is about to lose both his love and his country, as he has been neglecting his royal duties. The consequence of the king's practicing "tender airs" is that he lacks the strength to take up arms for defense, and he loses his kingdom to an invader. Finally he decides to put an end to his life by drowning. The cycle closes with one of the finest examples of George's terse poetic sorcery, "Stimmen im Strom" (Voices in the River). It renders the lure of the water and we hear the waves' promise of blissful dissolution:

> Lovers lamenting and laden with sorrow
> Come and seek comfort in our domain.
> Here waits enchantment and here will be healing,
> Words will caress you and arms will enfold.
>
> Coral-lined lips among concha-shaped bodies
> Swim in the watery palace and sing.
> Hair is entwined in the branches of seaweed
> Nearing and ever receding again.
>
> Torches creating a faint bluish twilight
> Hovering columns encircling the house,
> Waters like viols in tremulous motion,
> Rock you in blissful contemplative calm.
>
> But in the end, song and thought leave you weary.
> Slow-floating pleasure is stopped by a kiss
> And you dissolve into soft undulation,
> Glide as a wave up and down in the stream.

The water that entices to death is a variation of streams and fountains which the poet uses elsewhere as a mirror and a means to attain self-knowledge. Here it represents the allurement of death after the victim has attained self-knowledge and felt ultimate despair.

Regarding the whole of George's work from *Hymnen* to *Die Bücher* . . . we see that a close connection exists between the dream of kingship and the love of woman. Algabal moves in a void, exhibiting no truly human quality as a ruler or as a lover. His incapacity for love and the inhuman aspects of his reign caused his unhappiness and death. The owner of the "Hanging Gardens," however, is at first a successful ruler and a popular hero. In love he proves equally successful. His death is the result of the loss of both his kingdom and his love. He had fallen in love when his power was greatest. He lost his kingdom because his passion made him neglectful of his rule, and subsequently he lost his beloved. Both experiences, power and love, are conceived in the same terms; namely, they create relationships of inequality. The autocrat is the master over his slaves; this same power gives him the right to the most beautiful and chaste of women. At the same time, the terms of master and servant are, to a degree, interchangeable. In love, the "master" often assumes the attitude of the worshipping servant. This love degenerates quite frequently into servility. Likewise, George's minstrels and knights will do anything for their ladies, no matter how cruel and cold the latter may be. In George's hierarchical thinking, the relation between the sexes is based upon an initial plea by one partner and the possibility of a granting by the other. The alternative of a harmonious "give-and-take" hardly exists. Nonetheless the "Hanging Gardens" do contain an approximation of a more normal human attitude, both in the ruler's magnanimity toward the conquered and in the brief union with the beloved.

The next volume, *Das Jahr der Seele* (The Year of the Soul, 1897), has gone through more editions and has attracted more readers than any other of George's books. It was originally dedicated to Ida Coblenz; but the poet put an abrupt end to his friendship with her when, in 1895, she formed an intimate bond with Richard Dehmel, a poet whom Stefan George detested and whom she married eventually. The dedication of the *Jahr* was changed to the poet's sister whom Ida disliked.

While there are half a dozen poems in the volume which were written in direct response to the Ida-experience and while the book as a whole could be seen as a reflection of the experience of woman as a companion, an experience which ended on a note of resignation or even renunciation, the poet's own warning should be heeded. In the preface to the book he insists that "seldom are I and You so much the same soul as in this book." In other words, the book is not to be seen as a late-comer in the illustrious line of German love and nature lyrics from Klopstock and Goethe to the Romanticists and Heinrich Heine. These poems are not personal confessions, nor do they attest to a harmony between the poet and the forces of nature. If there is a dialogue between an I and a You (both of which appear on occasion in the plural), they are both fictitious, although authentic, subjects in the poet's consciousness to whom he has assigned their roles.

Likewise, the natural phenomena which we find in the poems are skillfully manipulated. They reflect nature as subjected to human interference. We are in a fenced park with a gate and benches. The beech trees form a shady avenue. And to our surprise, the "Year of the Soul" consists of only three seasons: fall, winter, and summer. The well-known opening poem is spoken in the form of an invitation, "Come to the park they say is dead . . . ," and the addressed is asked to see how the last flowers of autumn, far from being dead, can easily be shaped into an autumnal image. Whether the colorful remnants of the declining year symbolize individual memories of the poet or the obscure beauties of the *fin de siècle*, there is in any case a re-strained joy at the artist's discovery of beauty and at his ability to give it form. In another autumn poem the fruits are said to "knock" on the ground, that is, they do not drop on the ground as nature and wind would have it; rather they knock or tap on the ground with a purpose as a man might rap at a door.

Sad despair begins the winter section, "Waller im Schnee" (Pilgrims in the Snow), but we note again the distance from and the manipulation of nature in the use of language that is taken from human craft: the [snow] "flakes" are said to "weave a pale sheet" where the soul would be bedded. In the third part, "Sieg des Sommers" (Summer's Victory), rather tentatively and haltingly the poet fights his way through to a note of affirmation of the joy of living in and for the Here and Now. Among the symbols for the victorious summer there are "silver tufts" that form the trimming (as of a garment) on the meadow's edge.

Upon the "Year" follows, in the same volume, a large group of poems which are expressly occasional or directly addressed to friends. They are entitled "Überschriften und Widmungen" (Inscriptions and Dedications). The volume's final section contains the thirty-two "Traurige Tänze" (Sad Dances), which form melancholy variations on the themes and motifs evoked in the "seasons" of the soul, including the anguish of poetic creation and the overwhelming force of human longing. Characteristically, the poet does not allow the book to end on a negative note. In the last poem he can discern "the tender-breathing wind of distant land" coming as a "liberator."

It is surprising how quickly Stefan George's reputation grew during the second half of the 1890s, despite the apparent inaccessibility of his poetry. Conscious and careful management on the part of the poet is evident. After he had gathered around him a select group of talented young men who shared his tastes and ideas he decided that the time had come to approach a more general reading public. One means to this end was a number of favorably disposed articles (nine altogether) which appeared in well-known reputable journals between 1894 and 1900..The authors, to all intents and purposes hand-picked by the poet, included the poets Hugo von Hofmannsthal and Karl Wolfskehl and several Berlin University professors. A wide section of the intelligentsia was thus introduced to the "New Poetry."

Moreover, during these years George gradually shifted his point of view from his early cosmopolitanism to a more deliberate identification with German concerns. He saw his work as a continuation of the German literary tradition and regarded his mission as a peculiarly German one and himself as the chosen herald of a revitalized heritage which had lain buried since the early part of the nineteenth century. In 1896 Jean Paul Richter, by then a practically forgotten author, was enthusiastically acclaimed in the *Blätter* as an early proponent of the art-for-art's sake principle and as Germany's "greatest poetic power (not the greatest poet, Goethe is that)". In 1900 George, together with Karl Wolfskehl, published a selection of Jean Paul's work as the first in a three-volume anthology called *Deutsche Dichtung.* The rediscovery of the greatness of Friedrich Hölderlin in connection with the comprehensive scholarly editing venture of Norbert von Hellingrath was to follow during the next decade.

George's constant traveling between Berlin, Munich, Frankfurt, Vienna, and Heidelberg demonstrates the care and devotion with which he cultivated multiple personal contacts. The result was the presence of Georgeans in the chief intellectual centers of Germany from around 1900 on. Anticipating the moment when his stature would be recognized, George said bluntly to Hofmannsthal in 1897, "For, as you know, not to seek success is great; to seek and not achieve it, indecent."

Der Teppich des Lebens und die Lieder von Traum und Tod, mit einem Vorspiel (The Tapestry of Life and the Songs of Dream and Death, with a Prelude, 1900) reveals the new stance in all its aspects, especially in the *Vorspiel.* This is a cycle of twenty-four poems of four quatrains each, strictly

[30]

identical in form. The composition is austere and the diction solemn. It is conceived as an inner dramatic dialogue between the poet and "a naked angel" who is the messenger of *das schöne leben* (to be paraphrased, perhaps, as "the nobly beautiful life"). The Christian dogma of man's redemption had lost validity for George, and the concept of the tragic life of unredeemed modern man was equally unacceptable. However, the poet became convinced that he was an especially chosen instrument of a spiritual power whose will he carried out when he charged himself with the task of creating a new quality of life. The sudden appearance, in the first poem, of the messenger from *das schöne leben* suggests that the concept is something the poet had known before and is not a new revelation; it is his own formulation. God, or a god, as the source of the angel's authority is not mentioned in the *Vorspiel*. The absence of any invocation before the messenger's appearance indicates the fact that he represents the poet's alter ego. The biblical image of Jacob wrestling with the angel is used to express the poet's possesssing himself of spiritual power and enthusiasm for his mission: "I will not let you go unless you bless me" (poem II, last line).

The "beautiful" life is to be lived here and now; it is akin to the Greek *kairos*, the opportune moment which is to be realized in this earthly life or not at all. It is a matter of being, not of becoming. The quality of life to be led by those seized by the ideal is dependent on their aristocratic predisposition or instinctive nobility. The adherent must rise above the currents or conflicts of contemporary life and shun such readily available modes of life as Christianity, the pursuit of scientific-materialistic progress, or even the "small band" that professes to imitate the ancient Greeks. Although George's love of the south and its clarity of thought and climate was never to cease, he now heeded the angel's command to love the "fields and winds" of the homeland.

The *schöne leben* involved an intense cultivation of personality. The great task of the poet is to impart the message to the circle of his disciples. Within this *Kreis*, careful distinctions of spiritual rank and maturity were made. However, the hierarchic structure was not embodied in anything resembling a dogma or set of rules. It was expected that the disciples would give allegiance to the poet-prophet as unwaveringly as he followed the angelic command; but his guidance was as informal as that of the peripatetic philosophers.

Despite the new focus on his German spiritual ancestors, Stefan George did not fail to honor the great luminaries of the Western tradition as a whole. The national and cosmopolitan aspects of his mission were seen as correlative; in fact, George and his followers shared the conviction that a regenerated Germany would lead a European cultural revival. Hence the poets of ancient Greece, Shakespeare, Petrarch, and Dante are apostrophized in the thirteenth poem of the *Vorspiel*.

The opening poem of the central part of the book, "Der Teppich" (The Tapestry), offers a clue to the complexity and difficulty of the task with which George finds himself faced when he attempts to interpret existence. For him the meaning of the pattern is hidden and enigmatic, discernible only at rare moments and only by the elect:

> Hier schlingen menschen mit gewächsen tieren
> Sich fremd zum bund umrahmt von seidner franze
> Und blaue sicheln weisse sterne zieren
> Und queren sie in dem erstarrten tanze.
>
> Und kahle linien ziehn in reich-gestickten
> Und teil um teil ist wirr und gegenwendig
> Und keiner ahnt das rätsel der verstrickten . .
> Da eines abends wird das werk lebendig.

Da regen schauernd sich die toten äste
Die wesen eng von strich und kreis umspannet
Und treten klar vor die geknüpften quäste
Die lösung bringend über die ihr sannet!

Sie ist nach willen nicht: ist nicht für jede
Gewohnte stunde: ist kein schatz der gilde.
Sie wird den vielen nie und nie durch rede
Sie wird den seltnen selten im gebilde.

(Here men are intertwined with plants and beasts,
Strange, but enframed within a silken fringe,
And azure crescents, milk-white stars adorn
And cut across them in their frozen dance.

And simple lines traverse a rich design
And parts are juxtaposed in crass confusion
And no one disentangles the enigma . .
Until one evening it springs to life.

In awe the branches, dead so long, now move,
The figures tightly held by strokes and curves
Now clearly step before the knotted tassels,
Presenting the solution which you pondered!

It will not come when bidden, nor observe
A wonted hour: nor be owned by guilds
Or multitudes. No words will give the key.
The chosen who discern the plan are few.)

During the late 1890s Stefan George was attracted to two
men: Ludwig Klages and Alfred Schuler, who together with
Karl Wolfskehl formed the so-called *Kosmische Runde* (Cosmic
Round) and who believed that intellectualism (*Geist*) was the
soul-destroying evil of modern civilization. Schuler presented
himself as a clairvoyant reincarnation of an ancient Roman
and lectured on the Eternal City. Klages, philosopher, graph-
ologist, and racist, based his ideas for a return to a Teutonic,

primitive, pre-Christian creed on some of Johann Jakob Bachofen's writings on matriarchy. In the long run George had no use for occultism. The relationship to Klages and Schuler cooled gradually until George precipitated a complete break early in 1904, but Karl Wolfskehl and George remained close friends the rest of their lives.

The so-called Maximin-experience of 1904 and its poetic transformation was George's answer to the Cosmics. In the spring of 1902 George met an attractive fourteen-year-old boy with a radiant personality and a gift for poetry. His name was Maximilian Kronberger and he attended the Maximilian-Gymnasium at Munich. We have an account of his friendship with the poet, as recorded by the boy in a sober and business-like manner in his posthumously published diary. A fatal attack of meningitis put an end to his life in April, 1904. It was a terrible blow to George who, in a letter to a friend, wrote of "the crushing end: I mourn an incomprehensible and early death which almost led me, too, to the last abyss." The encounter soon underwent a poetic transformation. The impression the boy made on the poet must have been profound, for George and some of his disciples did not hesitate to compare this experience to Dante's encounter with Beatrice and Hölderlin's with Diotima. Maximilian Kronberger was renamed Maximin. A slim memorial volume containing poems by the Master and members of the circle as well as some of Kronberger's own was published in 1906. The first sentence of George's *Vorrede* (Preface) sets the Dantean tone: "We had just surpassed the midday height of our life and we were anxious as we contemplated the near future." The unself-conscious nobility and natural simplicity of the youth appeared to be a divine embodiment of *das schöne leben*, now also referred to as *das neue leben* [!]. The death of the youth is seen as tragic

[34]

but meaningful. During his short earthly existence he had lived the exemplary "beautiful" life. He was transfigured into the god whose reembodiment appears only "once in every epoch." George saw himself as the divine youth's prophet and thus finally as the sanctified poet and seer of his age. The strange mythological creation of a spiritual son whose servant and "son" George has now become is contained in the twenty-two poems which form the central cycle or ring of the seven parts of the volume entitled *Der Siebente Ring* (The Seventh Ring, 1907), George's seventh volume of poetry.

The Maximin myth alienated many of George's admirers and scandalized those who had been indifferent. His Dutch friend, the poet Albert Verwey, was shocked and rejected it as an extremely German idea, while admitting that the poetry was a magnificent tour de force. Rudolf Alexander Schröder protested bitingly against the blasphemous undertaking of creating a "boy mediator." It is true, however, that George never attempted to persuade others to make the deified Maximin a part of their personal beliefs.

One of the facts which shows that the deified Maximin is an abstraction is the organization of the poems in *Der Siebente Ring*. The core, that is, the fourth "ring" or group of poems, speaks of the advent, death, and transfiguration of the god. The preceding third group of twenty-one poems forms the antechamber, so to speak, of the sacred central part of the book. It includes two poems that resulted directly from the "Maximin-experience," some that speak in general terms about love and passion, and eight fervently erotic poems which were actually written before George knew Kronberger, but now appear to be connected with him. The outer rings (the first and seventh), on the other hand, contain far less personal and esoteric matter. The first ring is of quite general import, as its

[35]

title "Zeitgedichte" (Poems Addressed to Our Age) indicates. The most famous among this group is called "Das Zeitgedicht" and begins with the stern sonorous line, "Ich euch gewissen· ich euch stimme . . ." ("I am your conscience, am your voice . . ."). It is a direct address to the poet's contemporaries in which he calls them to account. He judges that they have wasted their vital strength while he, the poet, knows those things that will endure:

> Of dung and poison was your soul concocted,
> You spilled all that remained of precious sap.
>
> . . .
>
> What was of old (by no one seen) endures
> And youth and flowers laugh and songs abound.

In the poem "Nietzsche" George does not indicate that he owes anything to the philosopher but recognizes a certain kinship in outlook. He sees Nietzsche's greatness in his proclaiming the end of an old era. However, he pities him for his failure to formulate and put into practice the way in which the new was to be brought about. When he wrote the poem (in 1900) he felt he knew the secret of the new life and defined it as "constraint within a circle of love." An almost literal quotation from Nietzsche's *Versuch einer Selbstkritik* (Attempt at Self-Criticism) concludes the last of the poem's four resounding eight-line stanzas: ". . . this new soul was/ Not meant to speak but should have sung instead."

The seventh and last ring is composed of similarly outward-directed, mostly short gnomic poems addressed to contemporaries or praising historic places and personages. The sixth cycle, entitled "Lieder," will be referred to below in connection with a similar group of "Songs" in George's last volume of poetry. Between that and *Der Siebente Ring*, however, there was *Der Stern des Bundes* (The Star of the Covenant, 1913), the book which, together with Goethe's *Faust*, German soldiers allegedly carried in their knapsacks as they went to war in 1914.

It is important to realize that the majority of George's poems from now on are didactic "State" poetry and that the Maximin myth inspires and directs especially the gnomic poetry of *Der Stern des Bundes*, his most rigidly formal cycle of poems. It has precisely 100 poems, totaling 1000 lines, and is subdivided into an introduction (nine poems), three "Books" of thirty poems each, and a "Schlusschor" (Final Chorus). However esoteric and cryptic they may appear at first sight, they are poems, not a breviary; that is, their value does not depend on the relative merit of the cult they serve. The first section, "Eingang" (Introit), deals with the god and what he did for and through the poet. Echoes of the biblical creation-myth are mingled with classical allusions:

> Let misty vapour take on clustered form!
> Let silver feet emerge from purple waves!
> Thus from our fervent conjurations
> The painful cry broke through and reached the living core.
>   (No. 6)

The "First Book" is about the poet, his past, his work, his manifold functions, and his relationship to his contemporaries, friends ("helpers of yore," before the advent of Maximin), and the "Cosmics." The "Second Book" treats specifically the poet's insight into the characters and problems of his close friends, after Kronberger's death. In each of these poems the poet and the respective friend are engaged in a dialogue. No names are used. The new form of Eros is presented in connection with the idea of *geistige Zeugung* (spiritual procreation). Associations of men who devote themselves to this concept,

[37]

like the *Kreis,* are held to be more enduringly creative than men and women can be together. After Ida Coblenz only the painter Reinhold Lepsius's wife Sabine had a more than casual acquaintance with George. Some more motherly-sisterly figures enjoyed his confidence in later years, but on the whole women had no part in the "State," and while casual friendships and love affairs were tolerated marriage was practically tabooed. The irreparable break between Friedrich Gundolf and the Master came when Gundolf insisted on marrying Elisabeth Salomon. He had previously been prevented by George from marrying a Swedish girl.

The "Third Book" deals, in its first ten poems, with the meaning of spiritual rebirth and with particular aspects of the new nobility of the spirit. No. 6 warns the newly born to beware of romantic yearnings while in female company and to shun the seductiveness of sweet music, for both will sap the strength of the soul. A gradually hardening antagonism toward music, as being inferior to poetry, can be traced in George's development as it ran almost parallel to the rejection of women. On the other hand, a number of George's earlier poems attracted some notable composers. Arnold Schönberg, for instance, set the fifteen poems of the middle part of the *Hängende Gärten* to music for voice and piano in 1907–8.

The next ten poems represent the "laws" of the Georgean "State." No. 11 tells the young to be hard and forward-looking, to be prepared to act, and, if necessary, to use a dagger:

> Ye shall spit from your mouth all that is rotten
> And carry among laurel leaves the dagger . . .

No. 12 succinctly brands the asking or granting of forgiveness as abominable. The disciple must atone for great wrongs by learning from heroes to throw himself onto his sword and atone for small ones "silently by deeds." Among the body of George's dedicatory poems there are a few which commemorate young suicide victims.

No. 14 defines the three stages of knowledge: inborn, handed-down, and the wisdom that opens the gate to final initiation. However, the third stage is attained only by "those with whom the god has slept." Another version of the same idea is to be found in the 24th poem: "Ein weiser ist nur wer vom gott aus weiss" (paraphrased: "A wise man is only he whose knowledge stems from the god"). This is a rendering of line 154 of Pindar's second Olympic Ode ("Sophos o polla eidos phya"). It is significant that George says "god" where Pindar has "nature." It is not certain, however, whether he made the change with knowledge of the original or simply took it over from Tycho Mommsen's translation which Ernst Morwitz had brought to his attention. This poem and the rest of the last group of ten are poems of praise, all based on more or less veiled instances in the poet's experience. The 29th explains what happens to the disciples when they have reached maturity:

> You are dismissed now from the inner room,
> The cell that breeds the core of potent strength
> And pregnant showers. So go forth.
> The glance of each will tell his worth and rank,
> The form of each his kind of future daring.
> By separate paths you reach a common goal.
> The threefold wine of love flows in your blood.
> The fair of yesterday today are strong,
> Have grown through the Arouser's shielding care
> Whose smile and strength will radiate through you.

The beginning lines of this poem are a typical example of the ever-recurring biological imagery for the growth of the "new life."

Stefan George was convinced that the poet's dream was the

[39]

stuff that life could be made of. On the other hand, he insisted that he *could* have been a man of action. He is reported to have said to Robert Boehringer, "If at the age of twenty I had had 20,000 soldiers, I would have put all the potentates of Europe to flight." On the same occasion he said that he had completely overcome the temptation of letting himself be lured into the active life. Kurt Breysig has recorded a conversation of November, 1916, in which George stated that he would "certainly be able to turn to politics. . . . If, during the war, things should take a turn for the worse, and no better person was available to assume the leadership [i.e., the office of Chancellor], he would do it." The problem of the active life versus the poet's is the subject matter of the ninth poem of the first book of the *Stern*, where George alludes to the Greek poet Tyrtaeus whose songs stimulated the Spartan soldiers to deeds of heroism and thus helped win a battle. George never wrote or said anything that could be considered war propaganda. However, his thinking was more and more directed toward Germany's national and international problems. He saw far sooner than some of his younger friends (i.e., in the fall of 1916, if not earlier) that World War I was a disaster for his country and that defeat was a possibility. Yet he also believed in the necessity of war and prophesied that "tens of thousands" would have to be killed before the building of a new world could begin and that this might involve everybody in another world war. A poem which was published in 1921 as one of *Drei Gesänge* (Three Cantos) bore the prophetic title "Einem jungen Führer im ersten Weltkrieg" (To a Young Leader in the First World War). A young officer is addressed here as he returns from the war profoundly disillusioned, and the poet tells him not to regard the personal effort and discipline as waste of energy.

[40]

Drei Gesänge was incorporated into a group of fifteen longer poems that form the opening section of the last volume of poetry published during the author's lifetime, *Das Neue Reich* (1928, Volume IX of the first complete edition that was begun in 1927). This volume lacks the close cyclical cohesion of earlier volumes. Some of its poems were written as early as 1908, but included also are all those written after *Der Stern des Bundes*. The latter are not numerous but are weighty in some of their pronouncements. The first of the three cantos, entitled "Der Dichter in Zeiten der Wirren" (The Poet in Times of Confusion), is written in three stanzas of thirty lines of blank verse each. It has given rise to much debate concerning the degree to which George can be said to have prepared the advent of National Socialism. The poet compares himself with Cassandra and Jeremiah who warned their people of impending disaster and refused to dispense easy comfort. Like them he sounds like "coarse metal and is not listened to." George proceeds to explain his tasks as guardian and spiritual provider for his nation, especially its younger generation. He believes that after having gone "through deepest waste" the chosen ones will one day enable "the heart of the continent to save the world." The purified German youth will "measure men and things with genuine norms" and "bring forth the only helper, the Man" ("Den einzigen der hilft den Mann"), who will then "affix the true symbol on the national banner" and, at the head of his "loyal band," will plant the "New Reich." It is obvious that in this context "New" could easily be read as "Third," even if twelve years later the poet turned away in disgust from the brown reality which must have seemed to him a vulgar travesty of what he wanted.

There is no denying that George's assumption of the role of the prophet, pedagogue, and seer amounts to a monumental pose. There is, however, another, more private and relaxed side of his personality. Correspondingly, there are sections even through to the very end of his work which show less formal rigidity than the great cycles of state poetry. We find expressions of grief, defeat, and disillusionment in the end sections of *Der Teppich des Lebens* ("Lieder von Traum und Tod"), *Der Siebente Ring* ("Lieder"), and *Das Neue Reich* ("Das Lied"). A poem from the "Lieder" may serve as an example:

> In the wind's weaving
> My question was
> Only a daydream.
> Only a smile
> Was what you gave.
> Upon misty night
> Rose lustrous light—
> It will be May.
> Now I must live
> In yearning
> All my days
> For your eyes, for your hair.

Mistakenly many commentators (especially the hagiographers) insist that George adopted in his later years the tone, feeling, and form of the simple folksong. George's verdict on this type of the lyric genre had always been severe. In his anthology *Deutsche Dichtung* he omitted deliberately Goethe's and the Romantics' refashioned or imitated *Volkslieder*, and in 1902 he had remarked to Hofmannsthal that in most cases "their obvious silliness" is but thinly disguised through the interference of those who handed them down. In the exclusion of the folksong tradition from the realm of high poetry he remained consistent. One poem in particular implies a refutation of George's alleged adoption of the folksong tone. "Das Wort" (The Word, first published in 1919), in the group "Das Lied" of *Das Neue Reich,* manifests its nonsong quality in its structure of rhyming couplets as well as in the title. It is obviously not the musical connotation of *Lied* which explains the placing of this poem under such a group heading, but rather the store of motifs, stemming from legend, myth, or folklore, on which the poet draws. In "Das Wort" the poet speaks of his creative task as neither simple nor folklike, but as rather arduous. He has to pay recurrent visits to the "gray Norn" of Teutonic mythology, whom he must ask to give the name for every "new dream or wonder from afar" that he brings to his country. At the bottom of her well she searches for the name. Once it happened that she could not grant his request because she found that no suitable word was "sleeping in the depth":

> Thus I learned early to forgo:
> No thing exists for which there is no word.

The poem is both a supreme glorification of the poet's creative power and an acknowledgment of its limitations. A melancholy admission of ultimate frailty and subjection to unknown demonic forces prevails also in what is probably the last poem George wrote—it has no title:

> In stillste ruh
> Besonnenen tags
> Bricht jäh ein blick
> Der unerahnten schrecks
> Die sichre seele stört
>
> So wie auf höhn
> Der feste stamm
> Stolz reglos ragt
> Und dann noch spät ein sturm
> Ihn bis zum boden beugt:
>
> So wie das meer
> Mit gellem laut

Mit wildem prall
Noch einmal in die lang
Verlassne muschel stösst.

(Through stillest calm
Of pensive day
Falls suddenly a glance
Which stirs the soul that was secure
With unsuspected fright.

As on the ridge
The tree stands firm
Unmoved and proud
Until quite late the storm
Will bend it to the ground.

As will the sea
With one shrill sound
With one wild leap
Blow once again into
The long deserted shell.)

In the twenty-second poem of the *Vorspiel* the poet asks the angel if he will have to stand alone to the end. He receives the chilling answer that the disciples "love you, yet are weak and cowardly," and that at the close "only you and I" will remain. When George died years later in his self-imposed Swiss exile this prophecy was not literally fulfilled; a few close friends, both young and old, were with him. Among them were the two Counts Stauffenberg. Claus Schenk, the younger of the two brothers, was the man who planted the bomb in Hitler's field headquarters on July 22, 1944. Many Germans consider this much celebrated deed the most important act of the German Resistance. It is said to have saved their "honor" and re-established the moral stature of George and his followers as the true stewards of the "secret Germany."

In determining Stefan George's rank as a poet, however, one must not judge his achievements solely by their social and political irradiation, certainly not by the fact that history has ridden roughshod over the dream of the "New Reich." Among modern German poets there are very few indeed who would deny that they owe a debt to this consummate expert in the craft of poetry, an inspired, if stern, rejuvenator of the German poetic language.

SELECTED BIBLIOGRAPHY

NOTE: *The bibliography of Stefan George and his Circle by G. P. Landmann (see below) is a well-nigh complete annalistic arrangement of 1,512 items covering the years 1890 to 1960. U. K. Goldsmith's bibliography in* Stefan George: A Study of His Early Work *(1959) is alphabetical, but less complete. For the last nineteen years the editors of the periodical* Castrum Peregrini *(Amsterdam) have published bibliographical addenda to keep Landmann up to date. The secondary literature listed here comprises items relevant to a general understanding of the poet's work and includes those to which the present author feels especially indebted.*

THE WORKS OF STEFAN GEORGE

Gesamt-Ausgabe der Werke. Endgültige Fassung. Vols. 1-18. Berlin, 1927-34.

Werke. Ausgabe in zwei Bänden. 2d ed. Munich and Düsseldorf, 1968.

Correspondence

George, Stefan, and Friedrich Gundolf. Briefwechsel. Düsseldorf, 1962. 400 pp.

George, Stefan, and Hugo von Hofmannsthal. Briefwechsel. 2d enl. ed. Düsseldorf, 1953. 272 pp.

George as Editor

Blätter für die Kunst. Eds. Carl August Klein and Stefan George. 12 vols. Berlin, 1892-1919. Reprinted Düsseldorf, 1967.

Deutsche Dichtung. Eds. Stefan George and Karl Wolfskehl. 3 vols. I, Jean Paul; II, Goethe; III, Das Jahrhundert Goethes. Berlin, 1900, 1901, 1902.

Translations of George's Works

Choix de poèmes. Trans. Maurice Boucher. 96 poems, bilingual. 2 vols. Paris, 1941 and 1943.

The Works of Stefan George. Trans. Olga Marx and Ernst Morwitz. Chapel Hill, 1949. 348 pp.

CRITICAL WORKS AND COMMENTARY

Aler, Jean Matthieu Marie. Im Spiegel der Form: Stilkritische Untersuchungen von Stefan Georges Maximindichtung. Amsterdam, 1947. 304 pp.

Bock, Claus V. Wortkonkordanz zur Dichtung Stefan Georges. Amsterdam, 1964. 759 pp.

Boehringer, Robert. Ewiger Augenblick. 2d ed. Düsseldorf, 1965. 63 pp.

——. Mein Bild von Stefan George. 2 vols. 2d enl. ed. Düsseldorf, 1967. 316 + 195 pp.

Breysig, Kurt. Stefan George: Gespräche, Dokumente. Amsterdam, 1960. 112 pp.

Curtius, Ernst Robert. "George, Hofmannsthal und Calderon," in Kritische Essays zur Europäischen Literatur. Bern, 1950. Pp. 172-201.

——. "Stefan George im Gespräch," *ibid.*, pp. 138-57.

David, Claude. Stefan George: Son oeuvre poétique. Lyons, 1952. 409 pp.

Durzak, Manfred. Der junge Stefan George: Kunsttheorie und Dichtung. Munich, 1968. 294 pp.

Goldsmith, Ulrich K. Stefan George: A Study of His Early Work. Boulder, Colo., 1959. 172 pp.

Gsteiger, Manfred. "Die Blumen des Bösen. Stefan George als Übersetzer Baudelaires," in Literatur des Übergangs. Bern, 1963. 173 pp.

Hildebrandt, Kurt. Erinnerungen an Stefan George und seinen Kreis. Bonn, 1965. 338 pp.

——. Das Werk Stefan Georges. Hamburg, 1960. 475 pp.

Kahler, Erich von. Stefan George: Grösse und Tragik. Pfullingen, 1964. 31 pp.

Klussmann, Paul G. Stefan George: Zum Selbstverständnis der Kunst und des Dichters in der Moderne. Bonn, 1961. 181 pp.

Kommerell, Max. Briefe und Aufzeichnungen, 1914-1944. Olten, 1967, 491 pp.

Kronberger, Maximilian. Nachlass. Zurich, n.d. (1937?). 71 pp.

Landmann, Edith. Gespräche mit Stefan George. Düsseldorf, 1963. 216 pp.

Landmann, Georg P. Stefan George und sein Kreis: Eine Bibliographie. Hamburg, 1959. 240 pp.

Landmann, Georg P., ed. Der Georgekreis: Eine Auswahl aus seinen Schriften. Cologne, 1965. 502 pp.

Michels, Gerd. Die Dante-Übertragungen Stefan Georges: Studien zur Übersetzungstechnik Stefan Georges. Munich, 1967. 279 pp.

Morwitz, Ernst. Die Dichtung Stefan Georges. 2d ed. Godesberg, 1948. 179 pp.

——. Kommentar zu dem Werk Stefan Georges. Düsseldorf, 1960. 486 pp.

——. Kommentar zu den Prosa- Drama- und Jugend-Dichtungen Stefan Georges. Düsseldorf, 1962. 120 pp.

Muth, Karl. Schöpfer und Magier. Leipzig, 1935. Pp. 133-95.

Salin, Edgar. Um Stefan George: Erinnerung und Zeugnis. 2d ed. Munich, 1954. 360 pp.

Schonauer, Franz. Stefan George in Selbstzeugnissen und Bilddokumenten. Hamburg, 1960. 177 pp.

Schultz, H. Stefan. Studien zur Dichtung Stefan Georges. Heidelberg, 1967. 207 pp.

Stolpe, Sven. "Stefan George"; "Gundolf," in Stefan George och andra studier. Stockholm, 1956. Pp. 11-132; 135-77.

Thormaehlen, Ludwig. Erinnerungen an Stefan George. Hamburg, 1962. 299 pp.

Urban, G. R. Kinesis and Stasis: A Study in the Attitude of Stefan George and his Circle to the Musical Arts. The Hague, 1962. 209 pp.

Verwey, Albert. Mein Verhältnis zu Stefan George: Erinnerungen aus den Jahren 1895-1928. Trans. from the Dutch by Antoinette Eggink. Strasbourg, 1936. 89 pp.

Vordtriede, Werner. "The Mirror as Symbol and Theme in the Works of Stéphane Mallarmé and Stefan George," *Modern Language Forum*, XXXII (1947), 13-24.

Winkler, Eugen Gottlob. Dichtungen, Gestalten und Probleme, Nachlass. Pfullingen, 1956. (Esp. pp. 221-35 and 360-64.)

Wolters, Friedrich Wilhelm. Stefan George und die Blätter für die Kunst: Deutsche Geistesgeschichte seit 1890. Berlin, 1930. 590 pp.

Zeller, Bernhard, ed. Stefan George, 1868-1968: Der Dichter und sein Kreis. Munich, 1968. 421 pp. (Descriptive catalogue of the Marbach exhibition.)